DESTINY

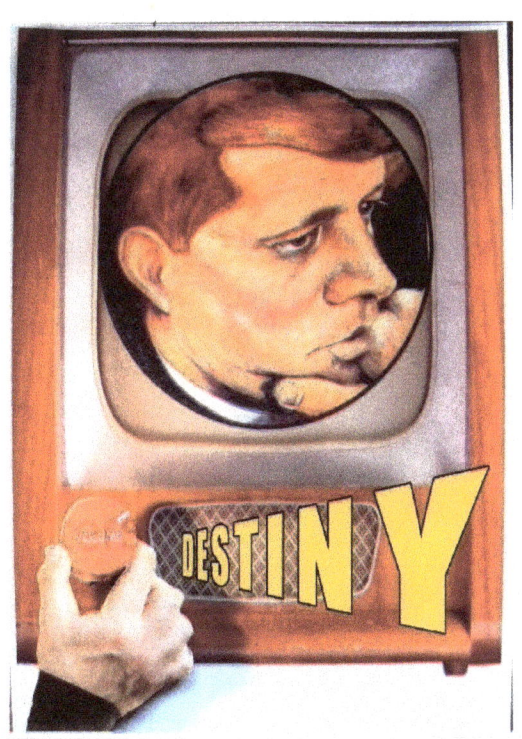

Peter Dyer

DESTINY?
DESTINY?
DESTINY?

Do you believe in Destiny?
Do you believe that all your actions,
All what you become, your life,
Was planned, maybe before the Universe began.
Looking for answers in this book?
The author regrets that, you probably will not.
This is a journey, you may travel alone.
But then again,
there is one who knows the route.
PRD

To my beloved parents
Elizabeth and Edward

Mouse Gate Press
1103 Middlecreek
Friendswood, Texas 77546
281-992-3131 TEL
www.mousegate.com

All rights reserved. Except as permitted under the United States Copyright Act of 1976, No part of this publication may be reproduced, stored in a retrieval system, or transmitted in any form or by any means electronic or mechanical or by photocopying, recording, or otherwise without prior permission of the publisher. Exclusive worldwide content publication / distribution by TotalRecall Publications, Inc.

Copyright © 2025 By: Peter D.
Cover Art and Illustrations: Peter Dyer
Technical Production by: Charles the PC Guy.

All Rights Reserved
ISBN: 978-1-64883-291-8
UPC: 6-43977-42918-2

FIRST EDITION
1 2 3 4 5 6 7 8 9 10

The scanning, uploading and distribution of this book via the Internet or via any other means without the permission of the publisher is illegal and punishable by law. Please purchase only authorized electronic editions, and do not participate in or encourage electronic piracy of copyrighted materials. Your support of the author's rights is appreciated.

I Wished You Nearer 1
Mirror Mirror.. 3
Energy of A Rocketeer... 5
Walk You Now A Lonely Road?... 6
Pings Are What They Used To Be. 8
Look Up (Very) Carefully! 10
A View From A Tall Mast... 12
Last Mile Home 16
Is There A Time Machine In Your House? 18
The Price of Gaining Camelot 20
The Coal Gatherer 22
The Desk 24
Paid Fare.. 26
Paintings by the Author 28
    A-1. Memories of the 1950s:..28
    B-2. Out at First Base:..29
    C-3. THIS song HAS nearly ENDED:..................................30
    D-4. The Departure:..31
    E-5. The Star of Hope: 32
    F-6. The Happy Harry Incident: 33
    G-7. Trees:..34
    H-8. Sunset Breaking Over the Ruined Chapel:................35
    I-9. The Stepping Stones: 36
    J-10. The Bridge:...37
    K-11. We Circled the Doomed Great Ship: 38
    L-14. The White Cat Speaks to the King of Trees:............39
    M-12. University School, Southport, 1886:.........................40
    N-13. The Seed for the Forest Fell from the Sky:...............41

I WISHED YOU NEARER

You lie still in my hand little friend.
It is the way I always wanted.
When you gazed at me, wistfully
A beak full of worms,
I wished you nearer.
As when I dug the soil,
You waited and watched.
I wished you closer.
When I told you of your splendour
Your head upon one side you puzzled me.
"Is this human actually talking to me"
It seemed you were thinking.
Around tree and bush you hopped unafraid.
Ah! You came nearer, but not too near.
You turned this garden into something
I can't say what, it defies words.
And so I have my wish,
As you lie unmoving as I found you,
In my shaking hand.
This is not that closeness that I wanted.
Now as I pass the soil over your blood red breast,
Though your garden is flora full,
Without your presence dear Robin,
It will now seem.... *empty*.

MIRROR MIRROR....
(BUT NOT ON THE WALL!)
Into which I gaze, each morning as I shave

Every day, year on year.
So now I sadly stare,
As to how I now appear.
Chromed rimmed glass
With slim fluted stand
The years have dulled
your shine.
Since you were placed
By my father's hand
Upon this tiled shelf.
To reflect that image,
Which fate decided
That his son would
cherish for such brief a time.

ENERGY OF A ROCKETEER

That fine shaped fin cut through my skull,
They said it pierced the inner brain.
That polished, embellished nose cone,
Boldly coloured red,
Severed an artery in my head!
Uncontrolled projectiles, falling from the sky,
Can do that, even to a passerby?
FINAL IMAGE: that of Rick,
What did he say, or try?
He was concerned, his frown expressed it.
A reminder no doubt,
When we made our mark that day,
In the shape of a mushroom cloud of grey.
Upon our school labs ancient ceiling!
We blamed it on the Space Race and the Russians,
And on innocent, be speckled classmate James.
Our treacherous retreat, living him in range!
By the rocket's burning shell.
And as my final thoughts ascended as that cloud,
Was this not just déjà vu?
Of that similar launch?
As that first streamlined, gleaming projectile was able,
To leap from its steel cradle.
Rather premature, but very stable.
Our later verdict on Richard's missing brow
He became our first space traveler.
Of this involuntary contribution, we had no compulsion,
But to blame it on an electrical malfunction!

WALK YOU NOW A LONELY ROAD?

There was no road,
Like the Highroad.
With a route straight and true.
There was a traveller who walked its way,
His name? Only you can say.

But this Highroad was a short road,
Of that he did not know,
Until ahead loomed the "ROAD UP" sign,
Its cursed warning "This route to you is blind."

So at that crossroad the traveller took the Low Road,
You know the type your given.
Cracked surface, pothole striven.
Twisting, turning, unforgiving.
Welcome traveller to the Low Road.
No turning back.

Our traveller now glanced the view ahead.
A solitary streetlamp yellow glowed.
Stood beneath, a vested road man.
His torch beam showed, a cavernous yawning ditch.

The road man gestured sideways, slow.
The torches beam unmasked mud holes glowed,
Into one gaping mouth the traveller nearly fell.,
But the road man caught his arm and said,
"Don't be afraid, all will be well."

With a blackened hand he passed the beam.
From beneath his helmet whispered,
"This is your road my friend, second left, the one."
So the traveller left the unknown road and turned to wave.
But both road man and the light were gone.

"This is not my Highroad" he thought
"The one I once securely trod.
I do not know where it will make me roam.
But with the road man's beam and God,
Maybe, just maybe, I will make it home."

PINGS ARE WHAT THEY USED TO BE.
BY I-PHONE

"Mum I am sorry, they sent me home from school and I am really in trouble."

Don't worry Sharon we can soon.

(PING!) Hold on a minute dear, this may be important.

"Yeah! I know just, just want to explain, I know I forgot but the hospital said...."

(PING! PING!) Right, just a moment while I handle this call, been waiting for it all day. Get yourself a coffee from the machine.

"Didn't think you would come and pick me up, not after what we said to each other yesterday. "

"Get in the car for Christ's sake, do you think I have got all day....."

(PING! PING! PING!) hello! yes, yes I am on my way for heaven's sake, no you don't need to go on............

"Well here we all are at last. Boy, it seems like ages since we all......" (PING! PING! PING!) I will just have to answer that, the vet will be needing to report on Sandy.........

"But darling, Sandy has been dead for 5 years now, can't we at least talk about........

David please put that away for just this meal....."

(PING! PING! PING! PING!) Whoops there she goes again. Probably the office better just.......

no don't leave darling won't be just a .....

down three points already my God that is serious.

No! No! What else......

"So I went to the school and they said that Sharon has not attended for 3 weeks. I am worried especially after the marks on her...........

(PING! PING! PING! PING!) Hold on for a second. Bill what was the score? I told you the new centre forward looked promising. The next match, sure we can.............

"Can you not pay me some attention for at least a few minutes. I have not learnt to speak yet, not that it matters. My crying just annoys you. Can't you put that strange thing in your hand away for me. I lie here and all I here is that P P P....."

No my child you have entered the world of PING and I own it.

"You think so! Don't get too used to that supposed power you so wield over my mum, dad, brothers, sisters, aunts, uncles, friends, enemies......

When I get out of this pram, I have a power that you have never dreamed of and PING will be the THING which never again will RING!"

LOOK UP (VERY) CAREFULLY!

Lottery winner 1,295 lay on a Caribbean shore,
Stretched naked on the warming sand,
Beneath a blazing tropical haze,
Azure blue, vermilion, an ocean endless to the gaze.

Careless now to that shit world of finance,
To endless text and calls,
Number 1,295 had the answer,
Be caressed by the tropic of Cancer!

Fate had decreed that of all the million numbers,
Of all the those hope and baseless dreams,
Fortune stated all worries and pressures for 1,295 expired,
Replaced, with dreams every human being desires.

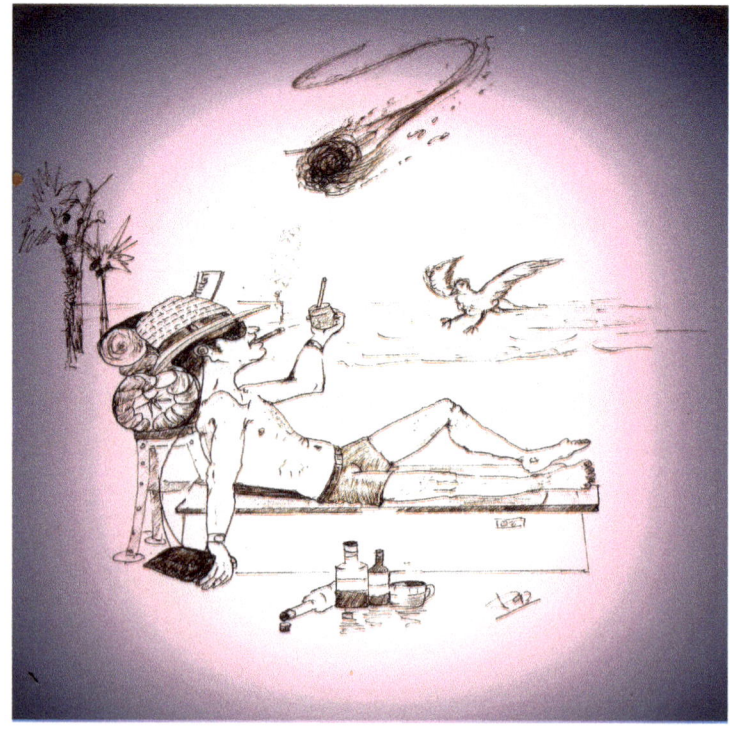

BUT

Above those swaying, coconut infested palms,
Above that thin white haze of heat,
One hundred miles circling this tranquil, idyllic scene,
There plotted a dark force, unseen.

Once the product of Man's deep scientific skills,
A device blessed by its inventors with countless gifts,
This gleaming metallic genius of space exploration desire,
Now returning to earth uncontrolled, a ball of fire.

Number 1,295 lifted a third Pina Colada to eager lips,
The heat on that plunging rounded sphere now turned to white,
Bare brown toes now caressed sand of exquisite texture to skin.
A strange increasing light, danced upon the dark glasses rim.

That shape of solid glow, split into a thousand splinters,
Now fate, that prince of fortune, removed its true mask.
A spear of sparks, once one of the satellites aerials, now breached
A scorching path towards that heavenly island beach.

Was it a sense of approaching doom made 1,295 awake?
To sit, to stretch, to taste a hypersonic wine not in the glass!
Then even worse, fortune raised 1,295 NEARLY to the feet,
What do you say when bronzed flesh and white metal meet!

Ah pilgrim, you are right, it probably wasn't much.
Hypersonic missiles don't really mess around with long speeches,
Even on the most Idyllic beaches.
And what was to be found of that person of great fortune fated,
A badly singed straw hat, within a crisp burnt wallet, a cheque…
Wrongly…. BACKDATED!!!!!

A VIEW FROM A TALL MAST

A sauntering gust of warm wind pushed the damp hair to the side of his tanned forehead.

There again was that familiar smell of his mother's scent, of an unknown origin.

Carefully, sensitively he stepped forward, bare feet caressing the rough Surface of the board.

The narrow, white plank appeared, in the Divers' imagination, to extend into an opaque void.

He was, however, not afraid as he had done this before from similar platforms in the sky.
Well just, perhaps, yes maybe this board did seem just a little higher,
Yes much higher than those others he had hurled himself from in his short life.
But the boy was confident there was no real cause for concern.
The firm, reassuring fingers of his coach now gripped his small shoulders.
Then they guided him forward while into his ear the voice of wisdom.
Those words had a semi hypnotic, soothing power.
This boy diver was never exactly too sure what power they had over his unconscious mind.
Indeed, he did not always focus too well on the detail of those final instructions.
But they came to him as the sound of waves running up a gradual shore.
Of the whispering autumn breeze, through apple trees.
The hands and the voice ceased.
The shadow of the coach would now retreat and then he was on his own. Well, not quite!
The coach put into the palm of his hand a small object.
It was a curled leaf from the apple tree. This act was their tradition.
As to its origin well this was only known to the young diver and his coach. It was a memory, a strange act of symbolism, echoing an event when he was even younger.
Now, with his toes sounding the board, at each step increasing tension crept up his legs.
It seemed to him a walk of a thousand miles towards this distant destination.
Often, he had skillfully climbed the aged, twisted bark of that old tree as the boy imagined it to be the mast of some great ship. That

view from its upper branches, he never tired of as it drew him back and back to their heights. There the sails thundered and the rigging screamed as the salt leaden wind heaved the great ship over.

Though the ocean pounded her without mercy with mountainous waves over rolling decks, she transcended their power to live again. Then the sun would dissolve into the west, setting the clouds and the sky on fire. On that day of days, as he made his way back down, the branch that bore his entire weight suddenly broke. He grabbed for the nearest branch, but his fingers connected to just air. Accept for that one, solitary, leaf. It was a strange event that followed, one which was to lead him to this high board on which he was now standing.

Instead of crashing into the ground, which would have caused his small frame some savage injury, something inside maybe, caused his arms to act like aerodynamic stabilizers, his knees to bend so they nearly touched his ears. The boy's body performed a near perfect somersault. He landed at the base of the tree on his feet, where he stood for a few moments completely DUMBFOUNDED!

Now he was staring down at that leaf gripped between his fingers,

Again, that distinctive presence of a scent of a once known origin. He tucked the delicate object into his swimming trunks, the end of the board beckoned............

As he positioned his toes over its edge. Silver water droplets cascaded from the board, plunging to the pool below.

For a moment his body relaxed, the voice of his coach had disciplined him to wait for just a few seconds before the airborne journey from the mast of the great ship. With eyes closed, his feet pressed hard against the board and then the diver was flying into the realms of space with swirling clouds and the hiss of cool air passing over his skin.

The diver awoke,
He was tangled in unwashed bed clothes and again became aware of the pain in his back. He examined the purple bruises which were a gift from those who enjoyed handing out such gifts and who had invaded that house he once loved. He stood up slowly and went to the window where outside, the view of a dark concrete estate stretching out in a carpet of urban desolation. White graffiti and a horizon dominated by distant high-rise sentinels. He turned to the stressed cupboard by his bed, the only suggestion of furniture. On its worn surface lay the gilded medals, their reflections dancing on an unpainted ceiling and by their side, a small pot. Within its dull glass, a pile of brown, ageing leaves. Swallowing, he lifted his favorite shining disc, running his finger over its not so polished surface. He hung it around his neck.
"Just one last time" he told himself through tear-stained eyes.
He picked from the pot the one last leaf that still was green. He tucked it into the palm of his hand and lay back on the bed closing his eyes. Then the sea returned, accompanied by a breeze that pushed aside the worn curtains. Invisible fingers touched his forehead.
These two agents of his dream had brought with them something he had never been too sure of, but now there was no mistaking their message. It was the voice of the coach. His father's measured words and tone lifted him back on to that high board and he heard every word that was said and perfectly understood. Now the hands guided him forwards once again and he felt the heat of the sun as it set the clouds on fire.

THE END

LAST MILE HOME

The traveller of oceans was stirred,
What was that so familiar presence?

A creaking of sea washed deck timbers,
The rolling of a freshly painted hull,
Cutting through a breaking wall of white foam.

Unfamiliar however, jumping from his bunk,
No sensation of vibration shaking her wooden walls.

Instead.... a strange, strange lightness.

It reminded him of when he was much younger,
When every day, was like a new dawn.

The voice from the vessel's cockpit,
Now, alerted his attention.

He climbed, his well-worn hat pulled over eyes,
Into the world he loved.

One of an eye watering and salt laced wind.

Above the towering mast, pointing towards a purple sky,
Gold early morning sunlight piercing racing clouds,
Reflecting on the weather-beaten smile of the Helmsman.

With an apology, the traveller clasped his firm hand.

"You should have woken me."

"No need, we have just one mile to go."

The Helmsman handed him the vessel's wheel.

As the traveller of oceans gazed towards the horizon,
There fell a windless calm.

But still the boat gathered speed,
Towards, the white light ahead,
A light which enveloped both boat and crew.

As that many sailed vessel dissolved,
The two guardians stood close, their voyage nearly ended.

"I never thought I would make it home."

Observed the seaman.

"You have always been here,"

REPLIED THE HELMSMAN.

IS THERE A TIME MACHINE IN YOUR HOUSE?
(OR LOOK IN THE ATTIC OR GARAGE FOR AN OLD DARLING YOU MIGHT KNOW?)

**CHECK NOW THAT IT WILL TRAVEL AT 33
AND ONE THIRDLIGHT YEARS PER MINUTE
OR THIS POEM AIN'T WORTH READING**

It might sit in your attic, purpose unclear,
Enveloped in thick dust, a layer for each year.
Walk to the engraved cabinet, once its wood was polished.
Inside lives the Time Machine, ah! those journeys were good.
Run your finger across the black disc, the source of its power,
A flight in the time machine? Less than an hour.
Flick that switch, will it still track?

Long Player thirty-three RP is about to take you back.
AND BACK! AND BACK! AND BACK!
Now the time machine speeds,
Just as it did yesterday,
That, song, that singer, that dance,
On goes the Time machine,
Measured in years not in miles.
With each turn of the disc,
Do you sigh, cry, but I hope as well you smile.
Your journey is over,
Pick up that magic sleeve,
Slide in the vinyl memory,
Time for you to leave.
Switch off the power,
Step back into your now.
But you will return,
Though you may never know how.

THE PRICE OF GAINING CAMELOT

When you reached for the screen of instant images,
That slick, gleaming man-made judge of past, present and future,
Was there once a moment, just one moment,
When its hypnotic screen bled into your mind,
A lasting image that even it could not control.
There rode in that slim, black limousine, on a cloudless day,
A weaver of dreams, a magician, one who,
Yes, could even bend that electronic master to his will.
HEY WATCHER
Did you see through with millions of other eyes,
How the smiling weaver of dreams,
For one last time, harnessed the glass screen,
To witness what had never been seen before.

Watch how that screen glides,
To catch the gaze of the President's eyes.
And in his final breath, did he recognise the crack of death?
In those final seconds, did he hear a muffled drum?
Hear the last heart beat of America's son.
As the very voice of his *DESTINY* spoke clear.
WATCHER
Did it not seem to those left to weep,
It was a heavy price to keep,
A final journey on a cannon cart.
Just maybe watcher, you cannot switch off the magician's dream.
What if nothing is really what it seems?
For his journey had only just started.
Towards his greater dream,
That mystical city of Camelot.
Even though the magician failed here on earth,
The Drawbridge of Camelot was lowered.
Beneath gleaming towers crowned with streaming standards,
Did it summon its son back to his real home?
Created before even time began?
A thousand silver trumpets vibrate a welcome,
From its high walls and to greet another of its heroes,
To take that still vacant seat at the round table.
Surely, only the greatest power in the Universe
Could return this knight,
From the savage, dark storm that once engulfed him,
Back to the Eternal light.

THE COAL GATHERER

Wander now across the sandy bar,
The distance to the breaker's edge, may not really be too far.
Even yesterday, it seemed, their rhythmic roar much nearer,
Was it an illusion, a trick of light, plunging waves no nearer?
The gatherer of coal pulled on his mud patched boots, an old friend,
To tread the tide worn tracks to this day's end.
Over uncombed hair, a faded cap, two sizes tight,
From beneath its peak, he viewed the circling gulls against the light.
As they climbed into the layered cotton cloud covered sky,
His mind spoke across the void to their unblinking eyes.
But there were no answers to his questions from the wind,
It just brushed with a familiar touch, his unshaven skin.
The route to the sandy bar was now a pathway of a running stream,
Its form reshaped by a tidal high which a few hours ago had been.
Marking his twisting route, white shell fragments, whole and broken,
"These, my many memories", he considered. "Seen, unseen and Many, many unspoken,"
Step over step he climbed the summit of that shifting mound,
Ahead, the ebbing, mud mixed power off the Estuary there found.

Stretching into view, the scattered remnants of an ancient seam,
A mystery to men, this source of nature's creation,
The presence of which, defied all explanation.
For centuries to warm the homes and bodies of both rich and poor.
Was this a gift, from countless broken hulls, upon the shore.
But it was the Gatherer of Coal who only knew the truth.
No vast Armadas of broken ships, failing mast or men.
Once he met a stranger, just the once, when he was a boy.
Lost in an arms-length fog of dense proportions.
On that day, he wandered so far his senses lost control.
A stranger appeared, grey bearded, white haired, weathered.
Without a word, he gestured for the lost boy to follow.
Closely the seeker followed the stranger, further than ever strolled,
To the edge of the limit where he thought oceans never rolled.
As the hissing breakers parted, they revealed a secret never sung,
An endless ridge of gleaming coal, created when the earth was young.
"How can this wonder have been so long hidden" he asked surprised.
"Ah!" laughed the stranger. "It has waited for your open eyes.
This wonder of nature will now hide beneath its sea cloak."
The young gatherer of coal walked into the foaming tide,
Small his fingers pressed down the nearest slithery, black sentinel.
Then, in a cloud of foam, it submerged from sight.
As many years weighed down upon bending shoulders,
He would still hear that stranger's laughter upon the breeze.
And in the drifting clouds unmistakable, the silhouette of that stranger,
As if projecting down, his departing words.
"Farewell, you are the Seeker of Coal and that is the safe way home."
The mist, the ancient seam and the stranger disappeared.
Just his sack, enough to carry, brimming with the black gold.

THE DESK

Bracing flat nailed hands upon the old familiar desk,
To steady the pain that filled his chest.
It was the old enemy within,
He knew it all too well.
More often now, he could tell.

Through dull glazed windows,
The sun's transparent rays,
They seemed to call his unsure gaze.
As if to say goodbye?

He moved his faithful pens in perfect line,
Yes, this would be the very last time.
Likewise a final locking of the draw,
The toiling years which had filled them, no more.

As a passing train, the discomfort seemed to fade,
Of increasing presence he was afraid.
The familiar folds of the office curtains were drawn,
There would be no new dawn.

He gripped the familiar fabric in some despair,
Dying light lit his well-groomed hair.
He turned coat on arm to leave,
The broad rimed hat from its hook retrieved.

It was then he became aware,
Of something in that darkened room was there.
A shaft of light pierced the curtain,
Of its origin, he could not be certain.
That beam for just a fleeting moment came to rest,
Upon those pens, lying on his desk.

Was it in his mind he heard say,
"As in the passing of night, there follows day.
Every curtain, however thick, can be open folded,
Into a once darkened room, new light rich rewarded.

PAID FARE

Is this a '56 Ford Consul?
That's right son, spot on.
Never seen one before as a taxi.
This is the only one.
Thanks for letting me sit in the front seat.
My pleasure, knew you would like the view.
You mean the spaceship mascot on the bonnet?
That's right, makes you feel like she is flying.
You think that too?
That's right my friend every-time, ever-time.
Not many taxi drivers know their passenger's names.
I do, everyone.

You know I can hardly hear the engine.
Well tuned boy, well tuned.
Are we nearly there?
Just turning into your avenue now.
I never forgot how the trees looked like a leafy tunnel.
Don't you worry, they know you are nearly home.
You know them, my mum and dad?
Very, very well. Here is the gate and its wide open.
The house, it hasn't changed a bit.
Neither have they, don't worry.
Somehow, I feel I have let them down.
I think you may be in for a surprise. There we are, I will open the door.
It is a bit of a drop for a small boy.
Is there a fare to pay?
No it's all paid. Better hurry there they are waiting for you.
Thanks driver, say have we met before?
We have many times. Run now, they can hardly wait.
He reached for the driver's hand and for a moment hugged him for something. It was then he noticed the scars on both his wrists.
"I think that was the longest journey I have ever travelled,"
The boy whispered in his ear.
The driver smiled," It was, journeys home are always the longest."
As the door of the taxi closed, silently, he turned to wave.
Now the passenger whose fare was paid,
Ran and Ran……

PAINTINGS BY THE AUTHOR

A-1. MEMORIES OF THE 1950S:
1987 oils on canvas/   Ford 1958 Mercury Phaeton Sedan

B-2. OUT AT FIRST BASE:

1999 oils on canvas/ owner Mr. K. Wilson North Carolina. (Painted when the artist was Little League Administrator for the UK)

C-3. THIS SONG HAS NEARLY ENDED:
1999 oils on canvas/ owner the artist.
(My favourite painting, a memory of my father on his walk a few weeks before he died of a heart attack when the artist was 10 years old.)

D-4. THE DEPARTURE:

2009 oils on canvass/ owner the artist.

The Foxmoth biplane used on the artist's hometown beach at Southport, NW England, prepares to take off. The passengers, however, have their own agendas.

E-5. THE STAR OF HOPE:

2010 oils on canvas.

A Victorian sailing ship wrecked on the Ainsdale sands.

F-6. THE HAPPY HARRY INCIDENT:
2012 Watercolour / Illustration from the author's book
[D.U.K.Ws](D.U.K.Ws) to WATER

Leaving the Irish Coal ship THE HAPPY HARRY. September 15th 1950 the crew of a Southport based D.U.K.W. leave the stricken schooner as a powerful storm gathers. The crew have spent all day securing the drifting and abandoned ship. Fortune was not, however, on the side of the UNHAPPY HARRY !!!

G-7. TREES:
2012 Watercolour /

H-8. SUNSET BREAKING OVER THE RUINED CHAPEL:
(2015) Watercolour / LYDIATE, LANCASHIRE.`

I-9. THE STEPPING STONES:

2018 oils on canvas / Kettlewell, North Yorkshire.
The artist nearly fell in while painting this one!

J-10. THE BRIDGE:
2018 Watercolour /

K-11. WE CIRCLED THE DOOMED GREAT SHIP:
2019 Watercolour / Illustration (unpublished) photo print.

L-14. THE WHITE CAT SPEAKS TO THE KING OF TREES:
2019 Watercolour /

M-12. UNIVERSITY SCHOOL, SOUTHPORT, 1886:
2022 oils on canvas /.

N-13. THE SEED FOR THE FOREST FELL FROM THE SKY:
2023 Watercolour /

Author(s) BIO

The Artist as a Young Man:

Self Portrait of the Author at 18,

He is wearing an American hat and Russian jacket

Peter Dyer was born, the last of 7 children, in the town of Harrogate in the county of Yorkshire, England. Peter's mother, on occasion, pointed out that the wonderful residence of that great county were well known for their uncanny ability to look after money. Peter, therefore, at times felt that perhaps God had made a mistake as this talent was not passed on to him. His mother pointed out that God does not make mistakes!

Peter moved to the coastal NW town of Southport in 1949. He went to a slightly eccentric private school, a stroke of great foresight by his father. From an early age our Peter appeared to be a little, well, eccentric or maybe different. He developed an early passion for space and rockets, both American AND Russian! (I am afraid especially Russian) This later led to building his own flying models and of course associated activity like explosions in the school lab, setting fire (twice) to the garden shed, interesting conversations with the beach Rangers. All part of a hobby that he was still practicing into the latter years. Peter showed a certain lack of interest in most sports, except swimming, especially CRICKET. At the age of 12, however, he discovered Baseball and by the age of 50 he became the English District Administrator for Little League Baseball UK. Well, all the best things take time.

Peter spent a few years at his local Art School discovering that, although he had some talent, it was not enough to earn a living and support his widowed mother. (His father died when he was 10). Thus, he became a Primary school teacher, for nearly 30 years. Peter also had a growing interest in historical subjects. American history, the civil war and that of the plains Indians in particular and also WW2. To cement this, he bought and restored a WW2 Ford/Willys jeep.

He has written 3 books on local history. His long-term strange fascination for the sea, heroic lifeboat tales, and consequently the exploits of the Southport coastal lifeguards, based on the American General Motors D.U.K.W. Recording these unwritten stories, taking nearly 7 years to complete, led to D.U.K.W s to Water. Recognition of these British Heroes, took an American publisher, after the author failed to find one after nearly 3 years of trying in the UK!

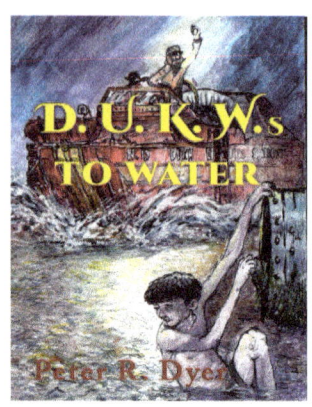

D.U.K.W.s to Water
- Author: Peter D. Dyer
- Publisher: TotalRecallPublications, Inc.
- Paper Back: ISBN: 9781590954706

What happened to the amphibious D.U.K.W. in its post WW II service. I hope you will find D.U.K.W.s to Water as fascinating to read as it has been for me to explore and to pass on to you.

The G.M.C. 6x6 Two and a Half Ton D.U.K.W. 1942

D=1942 U=utility K=Front wheeled drive W= Two rear drive axles

From the World War Two bloody beaches of Anzio, D-Day and countless Pacific amphibious DUKW campaigns, the revolutionary military vehicle, the GMC 6x6 two and a half ton DUKW became a legend forged in fire and war. Once the guns fell silent, the engines of the DUKW did not, as they found new waters, in a new role in a career that would bring them right to our doorsteps.

Unpublished archives now relate a fascinating story of courage and heroism on the coastline of Northern England, as the six wheeled amphibian, together with its crews of weather hardened Lifeguards, saved the lives of over 600 men, women and children over four decades. If that was not enough, the D.U.K.W. became a favourite with the public at large.

SHE IS STILL PLUNGING INTO THE WAVES TODAY
TAKE THEN A D.U.K.W. TO WATER!

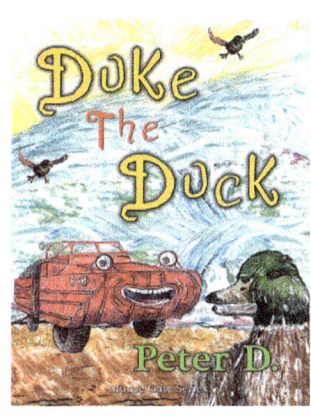

Duke the Duck

- Author: Peter D. Dyer
- Publisher: Mouse Gate Press.
- Paper Back: ISBN: 9781648830969
- eBook: ISBN: 9781648830976

In 2020 Total Recall Published Peter's detailed account of that rescue service in "DUKWs TO WATER." It was from that book that a new idea was hatched. The idea to make the D.U.K.W. into a character. This has been done before by mainly cartoon film companies and cars, trucks planes and even ships were just some subjects to be used as the basis for cartoon characters. Duke, however, represents a vehicle that is a legend from WW2 (reflected in the book) but saved and transformed. The author also decided, as the illustrator, that he did not see his story or characters as cartoons. Instead to try something more approaching reality and yet expressing a central hero who is a fantasy. Duke's adventures happen in the real world and he is surrounded by real people, not animated characters. Duke the DUKW and Mal the friendly duck also have one tire in reality and one wing in fantasy. The author considers that this ability to dwell in both worlds simultaneously is a gift that most children are given and YES it does remain with some adults as well!

DUKE THE DUCK is now launched. Hope it answers that nagging question...." So, just what is a D.U.K.W.?" Maybe soon you will be able to tell those folks at home or maybe those in your classroom and introduce them to the DUKE.

www.ingramcontent.com/pod-product-compliance
Lightning Source LLC
Chambersburg PA
CBHW061742070526
44585CB00024B/2775